Heinemann InfoSearch

The Outer Planets

Dr Raman K Prinja

Heinemann LIBRARY

www.heinemann.co.uk/library
Visit our website to find out more information about **Heinemann Library** books.

To order:
☎ Phone 44 (0) 1865 888066
Send a fax to 44 (0) 1865 314091
Visit the Heinemann Bookshop at www.heinemann.co.uk/library to browse our catalogue and order online.

First published in Great Britain by Heinemann Library, Halley Court, Jordan Hill, Oxford OX2 8EJ, part of Harcourt Education. Heinemann is a registered trademark of Harcourt Education Ltd.

Editorial: Nick Hunter and Catherine Clarke
Design: Jo Hinton-Malivoire and AMR
Picture Research: Maria Joannou
Production: Viv Hichens

Originated by Dot Gradations Ltd
Printed in Hong Kong, China by Wing King Tong

ISBN 0 431 15454 6
06 05 04 03 02
10 9 8 7 6 5 4 3 2 1

British Library Cataloguing in Publication Data
Prinja, Raman
The outer planets. – (The universe)
523.4
A full catalogue record for this book is available from the British Library.

Acknowledgements
The publishers would like to thank the following for permission to reproduce photographs:
Bettmann Corbis pp. **5**, **7**; Calvin J. Hamilton pp. **9**, **16**, **18**; Eliot Young / Southwest Research Institute and NASA p. **28**; NASA pp. **12**, **13**, **19**, **20**, **21**, **24**; NASA / Ames Research Centre / Rick Guidice p. **6**; NASA / JPL / Caltech pp. **4**, **10**, **11**, **14**, **15**, **17**, **22**, **23**, **26**, **27**, **29**.

Cover photograph reproduced with permission of Science Photo Library.

The author would like to thank Kamini, Vikas, Sachin and all his family for their support.

Every effort has been made to contact copyright holders of any material reproduced in this book. Any omissions will be rectified in subsequent printings if notice is given to the publishers.

Contents

Any words appearing in the text in bold, **like this**, are explained in the Glossary.

What are the outer planets?

Earth is one of nine **planets** that form our **solar system**. They all travel around the Sun in paths called **orbits**. The four planets closest to the Sun are Mercury, Venus, Earth and Mars. The other five planets are Jupiter, Saturn, Uranus, Neptune and Pluto. They are much further away from the Sun. These five planets are called the outer planets because they are in the outer part of the solar system.

Five fantastic worlds

Each of the outer planets is an amazing world with its own beauty and mystery. Jupiter, Saturn, Uranus and Neptune are sometimes called the giant **gas planets**. This is because they are mostly made of **gas**, and they are much bigger than the other planets. They don't have any solid surface to stand on.

Pluto is the most distant outer planet. It is very different from the giant gas planets. It is a much smaller, frozen ball of rock and ice.

Saturn's rings are enormous. They would almost fill the distance between Earth and the Moon.

Who first discovered the outer planets?

All the planets except Uranus, Neptune and Pluto can be seen in the sky just using our eyes. They have been known about since ancient times. Uranus, Neptune and Pluto are much fainter in the sky. Good **telescopes** were needed before these planets could be discovered.

Uranus was found by Sir William Herschel in 1781. He was a famous British **astronomer**. Neptune was discovered by John Adams and Urbain Le Verrier in 1846. Pluto has only been known about since 1930, when it was found by an astronomer called Clyde Tombaugh.

William Herschel was born in Germany but was living in England when he discovered the planet Uranus.

From largest to smallest

Jupiter is the largest planet in the solar system. It is so big that 1400 planets the size of Earth could fit inside it. Saturn is a little smaller than Jupiter. It has magnificent rings and lots of **moons**. Uranus and Neptune are like twins, because they are about the same size and are both a blueish-green colour. Pluto is the smallest planet in the solar system. It is even smaller than Earth's Moon.

A scale model

To understand the sizes and distances of the outer planets, try imagining this **scale model** of them. If the Sun were shrunk down to the size of a beach ball, Earth would be a large pea about 30 metres away from it.

Then in this model, the giant planet Jupiter would be the size of an orange about 380 metres away from the Sun, and Saturn would be the size of a tangerine. Uranus and Neptune would be the size of walnuts. Finally, Pluto would be a very tiny pea nearly 3 kilometres (2 miles) away from the beach ball.

This picture shows all nine planets in our solar system. The sizes of the inner and outer planets are shown roughly to scale. (The Sun is not shown to scale.)

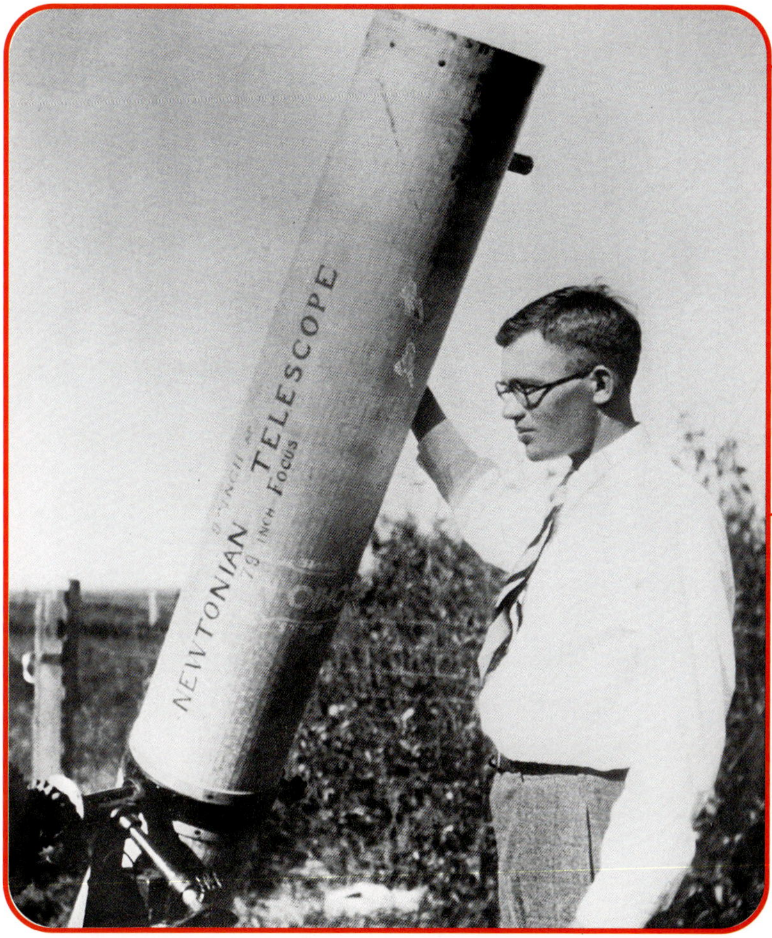

The furthest planet in the solar system, Pluto, was discovered by the astronomer Clyde Tombaugh in 1930.

Name that planet

All the outer planets are named after gods from Greek and Roman **myths**. Jupiter was the king of the Roman gods. Saturn gets its name from the Roman god of farming or agriculture. Uranus is named after the ancient Greek god of the skies. Neptune is the name of the Greek god of the seas, and brother of Jupiter. Since Pluto is so cold and far away, it was named after the god of the land of the dead!

What does Jupiter look like?

Jupiter is the fifth **planet** from the Sun. It is by far the largest of the nine planets in our **solar system**. Jupiter is often the brightest 'star-like' object in the night sky, and shines a cream colour. Venus is the only other planet that can appear brighter. You can even see some reddish bands or stripes across Jupiter through a small **telescope**.

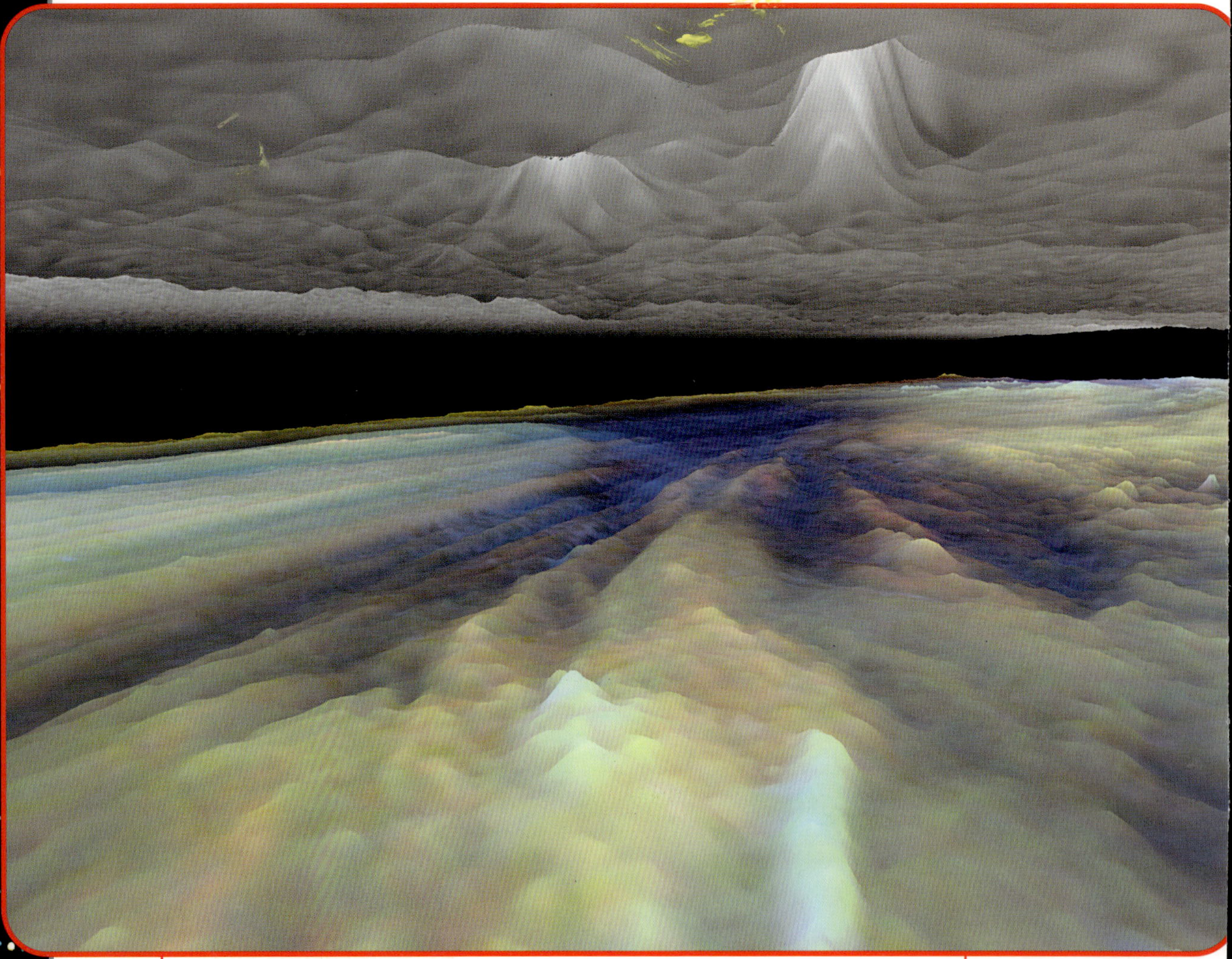

Jupiter's upper layers are made of swirling bands of different colours. These bands are made up of gases. They are constantly moving.

Jupiter is a **gas planet** which means it is mainly made of **hydrogen** and **helium gas**. Scientists think these gases turn into vast layers of liquid deep inside the planet. No one really knows if the centre of Jupiter is rocky or a slushy soup of matter.

A short day, but a long year

Though it's a huge planet, a Jupiter-day is only 9 hours and 55 minutes long. That is how little time it takes to spin on its **axis** once. A Jupiter-year on the other hand is very long. A year is the time a planet takes to travel around the Sun. Since Jupiter is very far away from the Sun, it takes nearly 12 of our years to complete its year.

None of the planets in our solar system are completely upright. They all lean different amounts and spin in different directions.

Storms and winds

From Earth, we can only see the coloured layers of clouds high in Jupiter's **atmosphere**. The clouds are too thick for us to see any further, even through powerful **telescopes**. The clouds make a swirling pattern of orange, brown, blue and white colours. Because the planet spins so fast, the clouds make bands of different colours, with high-speed winds of almost 640 kilometres (400 miles) per hour.

This fantastic view of Jupiter's Great Red Spot came from the Voyager 1 *spacecraft in February 1979. The Great Red Spot is a giant hurricane.*

Jupiter has an angry atmosphere that bristles with lightning strikes and huge storms. One of these storms is known as the Great Red Spot. It is an amazing giant **hurricane** that has been raging there for more than 300 years. The Great Red Spot is big enough to swallow up two planets the size of Earth.

Faint rings

Spacecraft sent from Earth have photographed dark narrow rings around Jupiter. They are faint and not nearly as spectacular as the rings of Saturn. The rings were discovered by the *Voyager* spacecraft in 1979. Jupiter's rings are made of tiny dust particles, and they extend out to about 130,000 kilometres (81,000 miles) from the middle of the planet.

This close-up view of Jupiter's faint rings was seen from the Voyager 2 *spacecraft in 1979.*

Does Jupiter have any moons?

The giant **planet** Jupiter has at least 28 **moons** that travel in an **orbit** around it. It is as though Jupiter has a mini **solar system** of its own. Some of these moons were made from the **gas** and dust that was left over when Jupiter formed. Many of the other moons were made much further away, and were captured by the strong pull of Jupiter's **gravity**.

Jupiter has four main moons, shown in this picture side by side.

The largest moons

In 1610, an **astronomer** from Italy called Galileo Galilei discovered the four largest moons of Jupiter. He was the first person to use a small **telescope** to look at objects in the sky. These four main moons are called Io, Europa, Ganymede and Callisto. They are named after the lovers of the god Zeus in Greek **mythology**. Each one of these moons has its own amazing story.

Io is the closest of the big moons to Jupiter. It is larger than Earth's Moon. Io has more **volcanoes erupting** on it today than any other planet or moon in the solar system. It has a very colourful surface because lots of yellow and red **chemicals** are spewed high by the volcanoes.

Europa is slightly smaller than Earth's Moon. It is covered by a thick, smooth layer of ice. Scientists think that Europa may have an ocean of liquid water under its icy surface. Astronomers think it is even possible that simple **microscopic** life forms exist in the oceans.

Ganymede is the largest moon in our solar system. It is even larger than the planet Mercury. Its icy surface is broken and split, with lots of criss-crossing grooves and bumps.

Callisto is larger than the planet Pluto and is almost the size of Mercury. Like Ganymede, it is also a very rocky and icy moon. Callisto has more **craters** on its surface than any other moon in our solar system. The craters are bowl shaped holes made billions of years ago when huge rocks crashed into Callisto.

You can see in this picture of Callisto, the many craters that mark its surface.

What are the rings of Saturn?

Saturn is one of the most beautiful **planets** in our **solar system**. It is the sixth planet from the Sun, and the second largest one. The planet appears in our night skies like an orange-yellow star. Saturn is famous for its dazzling rings, which can be seen from Earth through a small **telescope**.

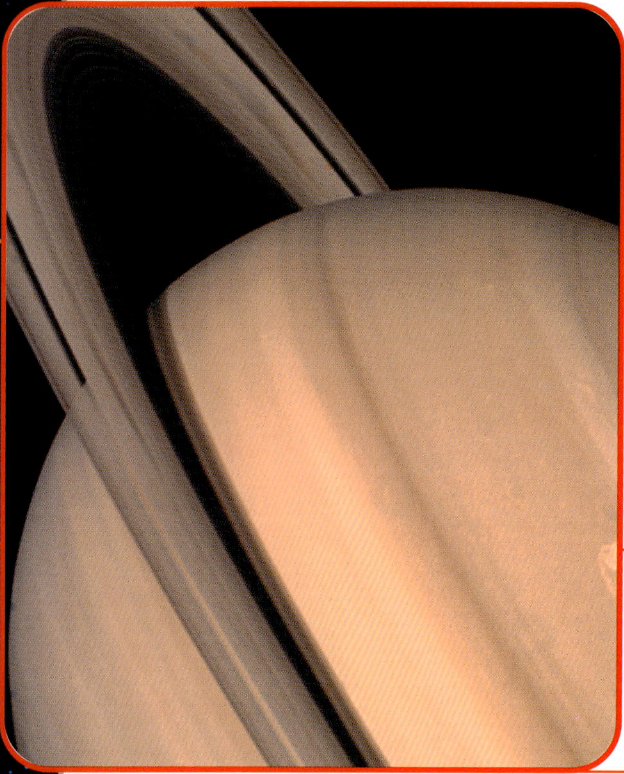

Saturn also turns very fast on its axis. Its day is only 10 hours and 39 minutes long. It spins so fast that it is slightly squashed, and looks egg-shaped. Because Saturn is so far away from the Sun, it takes over 29 of our years to finish one **orbit**. Saturn has a stormy **atmosphere**, with lots of lightning strikes and very strong winds.

Saturn's atmosphere has coloured bands, which are similar to the ones seen on Jupiter.

Who discovered the rings of Saturn?

The **astronomer** Galileo Galilei first noticed the rings of Saturn in 1610. He saw humps or 'ears' on each side of the planet through his simple telescope. Almost 50 years later a Dutch astronomer called Christian Huygens discovered that these 'ears' were really rings around the planet.

Magnificent rings

Measured from edge to edge, Saturn's fantastic rings are about 275,000 kilometres (170,000 miles) across. The rings are not solid, like a giant plate around Saturn. Instead they are made up of many different bands.

There are seven main rings, and hundreds of narrow ringlets, that circle the planet. They are made of bits of ice and rocks that can be the size of dust **particles** or lumps as big as houses!

Scientists are still puzzled about how Saturn got its rings. Some astronomers think they formed at the same time as Saturn, from material that was leftover and not pulled into the giant planet. Other people think that the rings formed much later. Perhaps they were made when a large **comet** passed too close to Saturn and was broken into pieces by the force of **gravity**.

A closer photograph of Saturn's rings shows how they are made up of many separate bands of rock and dust.

What are the moons of Saturn like?

Saturn has more **moons** than any other **planet** in the **solar system**. There are at least 30 moons **oribiting** it that we know of, and there could be many more small ones waiting to be discovered! Some of the moons formed at the same time as Saturn, and others were captured later by the giant planet's strong **gravity**.

This artist's drawing shows Saturn with eight of its largest moons. The planets and the moons are not shown to scale.

Strange little worlds

Many of Saturn's moons are puzzling. Several are covered with very smooth ice. One of them, called Lapetas, is as white as snow on one side and as black as coal on the other! Another moon called Mimas has a giant **crater** 130 kilometres (80 miles) across that was made when a huge rock struck and almost shattered the moon.

Mysterious Titan

Titan is the largest moon of Saturn. It is even larger than the planet Mercury. It is a strange and mysterious moon. A thick **atmosphere** of poisonous gases surrounds Titan. Scientists think that it also has lakes on its surface. They are not lakes of water, but of **chemicals** and oils. The lakes are a little like the oceans where life started on Earth billions of years ago. Exploring the lakes of Titan might teach us new things about how life first started on Earth.

How can we find out about Saturn's moons?

A **spacecraft** called Cassini was launched towards Saturn in 1997. It will arrive there in 2004 to study the ringed planet and its moons. Cassini is carrying a special smaller spacecraft called a **probe**, which will be dropped through Titan's atmosphere. The probe might even splash into one of Titan's lakes!

An artist's idea of the Cassini spacecraft getting close to Saturn and its moons.

How were the giant planets made?

Nebulae

The whole of our **solar system**, including the Sun, **planets** and **moons**, were made of **gas** and dust. These **raw materials** are found in huge clouds in space called **nebulae**. About 4 billion years ago, one of these huge clouds began to shrink under the pull of **gravity**.

Sun at the centre

Over millions of years a lot of material was squeezed into a ball in the centre of the cloud. The ball became hotter and hotter, and finally it turned into a star, our Sun.

Rocky planets close in

The gas and dust leftover was flattened into a spinning plate, or **disc** around the newly 'born' Sun. Close to the Sun, it was so hot that ice melted and light gases like **hydrogen** were pushed far away.

Only bits of rock and metal could survive close to the Sun. These lumps began to clump together growing steadily larger and larger. Finally, they formed into the four rocky **inner planets**, Mercury, Venus, Earth and Mars.

Neptune is billions of kilometres away from the Sun. Unlike the rocky inner planets, it has no solid surface.

Gas planets further out

In the outer part of the solar system, far away from the Sun, it was cold enough for lots of ice, dust and hydrogen gas to gather. The ice and dust clumped together, and slowly grew into giant balls. These huge balls then swept up lots of leftover gases, like hydrogen and **helium**.

They collected more and more gas, and grew larger and larger. These bodies finally became the giant **gas planets**, Jupiter, Saturn, Uranus and Neptune.

*The Space Shuttle takes **spacecraft** and **probes** out into space where they can explore and send back valuable information.*

Could I visit the gas planets?

All the giant gas planets would be very nasty places for humans to visit. There isn't any solid ground under the clouds for you to stand on. The **atmosphere** just gets thicker and thicker the deeper you go, until it turns from gas to liquid. The air is poisonous, so you wouldn't be able to breathe it. The gas planets also have fierce winds that would rip your body apart.

What does Uranus look like?

Uranus is the seventh **planet** from the Sun, and the third largest of the nine planets in the **solar system**. It is so far away that it takes 84 years to complete just one **orbit** around the Sun. Uranus can be seen from Earth with a small **telescope**.

Like Jupiter and Saturn, Uranus is a giant **gas planet** that doesn't have a solid rocky surface. It has a cloudy **atmosphere**, mostly made of **hydrogen**, with fast winds that blow at speeds of 600 kilometres (370 miles) per hour. Uranus has a green-blue colour, which it gets from a **gas** called **methane** in its atmosphere.

This picture of Uranus was taken by Voyager 2 *in 1986. It is hard to imagine the fast winds that are blowing on the surface.*

Rolling on its side

Unlike all the other planets in the solar system, Uranus spins sideways. It is tipped over, and moves around the Sun like a barrel rolling along on its side. Scientists think Uranus may have been knocked over on its side billions of years ago, when it was struck by an object the size of Earth.

Because Uranus is so tipped over, it has very long seasons. Its winters last 21 years, and the temperature near the tops of the clouds can be as low as –195 ° Celsius. In comparison, the winter temperatures at Earth's South **Pole** are about –60 ° Celsius.

Moons and rings too

Uranus also has **rings** around it. It has eleven faint, dark rings made of tiny bits of ice and dust. They look a little bit like the rings around Jupiter.

There are at least 21 **moons orbiting** Uranus. The strangest of these is called Miranda. It is covered in long valleys and steep cliffs. They criss-cross all over this odd-shaped moon. Miranda may have been shattered into lots of pieces in a giant crash with another object in space billions of years ago. The pieces were then brought back together by the force of **gravity** to form a new moon.

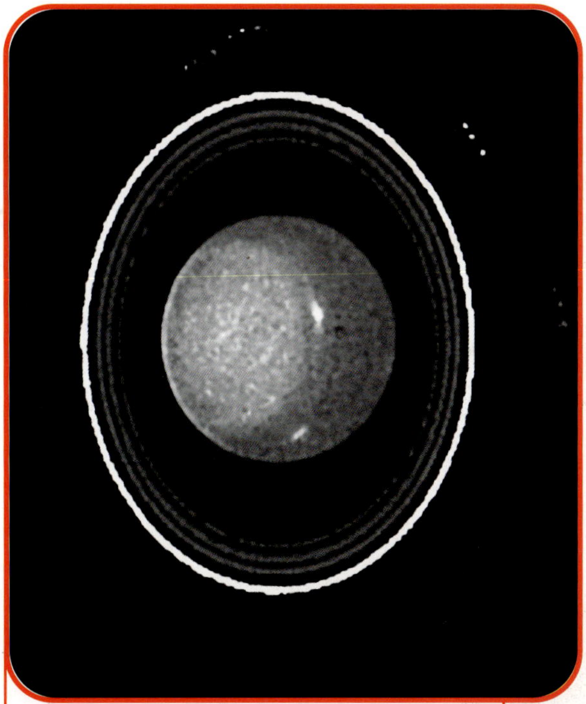

The rings around Uranus are very thin and difficult to see because they are made of dark rock and dust.

What do we know about Neptune?

Neptune is fainter than Uranus in the sky. It can only be seen through a good **telescope** or binoculars. It is nearly 4.5 billion kilometres (2800 million miles) from the Sun, and takes 165 of our years to go around the Sun. This means it will never finish one full **orbit** during the lifetime of a person on Earth.

Neptune is the smallest of the four giant **gas planets**, but it could still hold 60 planets the size of Earth inside it. It is mostly made of **hydrogen** and **helium gas**. Like Uranus, the planet gets its beautiful blue-green colour from a gas called **methane** in its **atmosphere**.

This beautiful photograph of Neptune was taken by the Voyager 2 spacecraft in 1989.

Fierce winds!

Many large storms have been seen on Neptune. The fastest winds of any planet in our **solar system** have been measured here. They can blow at speeds of 2400 kilometres (1500 miles) per hour. **Hurricanes** on Neptune can be seen as dark oval spots that look a little like Jupiter's Great Red Spot.

Neptune has at least eight **moons**, six of which were discovered by the **spacecraft** *Voyager 2*. The largest moon is called Triton. Triton has an icy surface where temperatures can drop to a freezing –235° Celsius. This makes Triton the coldest object yet discovered in our solar system.

The orbit of Triton is slowly spiralling in towards Neptune. Between 10 and 100 million years from now, Triton will crash into Neptune and break apart. When this happens, rings will form around Neptune that may be as magnificent as the rings around Saturn.

The faint rings of Neptune are seen in this picture from the Voyager 2 *spacecraft.*

Thanks to *Voyager 2*

A lot of what we know about Neptune has come from discoveries made using a spacecraft called *Voyager 2*. It visited the planet in 1989, and sent back pictures of several faint rings around the planet. The rings are made of tiny bits of ice and dust.

Why is Pluto different?

Pluto is the smallest and furthest **planet** in our **solar system**. Even through large **telescopes** it just looks like a starry speck. This tiny world is so far away, that it takes 248 years to finish one **orbit** around the Sun. Pluto is very different from the other outer planets because it is not a huge ball of **gas**. It is made of rock mixed with ice, and is smaller than Earth's **Moon**.

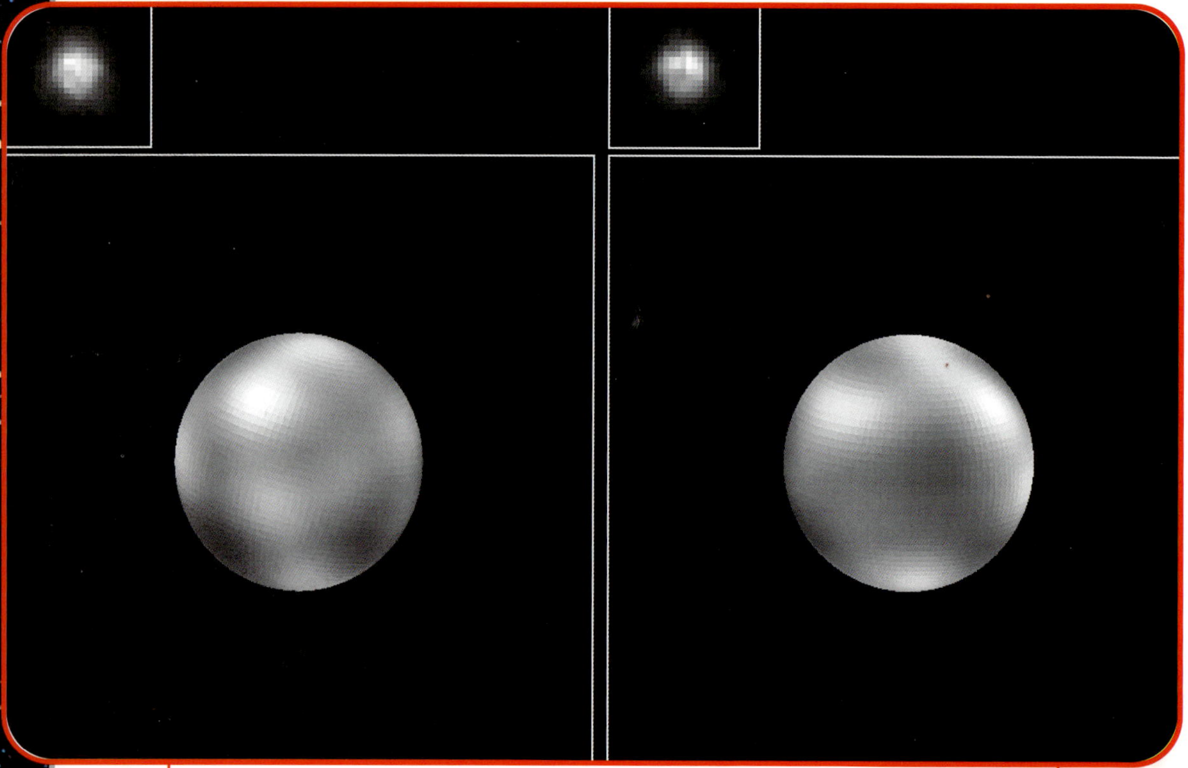

There are very few pictures of Pluto, and none that really show any detail. These pictures were taken by the Hubble Space Telescope. The Hubble Space Telescope is a very powerful telescope which orbits Earth in space and sends back pictures of stars and planets. The pictures in the small boxes (top) are from Hubble, and the big pictures are how ***astronomers*** *think Pluto looks.*

Another difference is that Pluto's orbit around the Sun is not circular, but egg-shaped or oval. Because of this unusual orbit, Pluto's path around the Sun sometimes crosses inside the orbit of Neptune. This happened between 1979 and 1999, when Pluto was closer to the Sun than Neptune.

A dark, frozen world

Huge, powerful telescopes have shown that Pluto may have ice caps on its **poles**, and large **craters** on its surface. Because it is so far away from the Sun, the temperature on Pluto can drop as low as –230° Celsius. Standing on Pluto's frozen surface, the Sun would only look like a very bright star does from Earth.

In many ways Pluto looks like some of the moons that orbit giant **gas planets**. Some scientists think that it may once have been a moon of Neptune, which escaped billions of years ago.

A tiny moon too!

Pluto has a moon called Charon. It is about half the size of the planet, and is mostly made of ice and rock. Pluto and Charon always keep the same face to each other as they travel together around the Sun.

Not yet visited

Pluto remains a mysterious planet. It is the only one that has never been visited by a **spacecraft** from Earth. Scientists are planning to send a **mission** to the planet called *Pluto Express*, which may get there by 2015. It would send back exciting pictures that could teach us a lot more about this distant planet.

How do we learn about the outer planets?

Powerful **telescopes** like the Hubble Space Telescope can be used to discover many new things about the **planets**. However, we have learnt most about the giant **gas planets** by sending **spacecraft** to visit them and to take photographs and measurements.

The *Voyager* missions

Two spacecraft called *Voyager 1* and *2* have visited and explored all four of the giant gas planets. They were launched in the summer of 1977. *Voyager 1* reached Jupiter in March 1979, and then went on to reach Saturn by November 1980. It also flew behind Saturn's rings and close to its giant **moon** Titan.

Voyager 2 not only flew past Jupiter and Saturn, but it also went to Uranus in January 1986 and Neptune in August 1989.

These amazing **missions** answered many questions about the giant gas planets. They watched storms, discovered rings and found new moons.

This drawing shows the Voyager *spacecraft exploring the giant gas planets.*

Galileo at Jupiter

In October 1989, the Space Shuttle *Atlantis* carried a new spacecraft called *Galileo* into space. It was sent on a long trip to Jupiter. *Galileo* went into **orbit** around the 'king of planets' in 1995.

The spacecraft has sent back fantastic pictures of storms on Jupiter and also of its moons. *Galileo* even dropped a small **probe** into the planet's unfriendly **atmosphere**.

Cassini to Saturn

A spacecraft called *Cassini* was launched toward Saturn in October 1997. It is due to arrive there in July 2004 and will spend four years in orbit around the beautiful planet. *Cassini* should teach us many new things about the dazzling rings and Saturn's amazing moon Titan.

Spacecraft missions have given us the most detailed views of the atmospheres of the giant gas planets. This view is of Saturn.

Fact file

Here are some important facts about the outer planets:

Size

Planet	*Compared to Earth*		*Kilometres across*
Jupiter	11	times larger	143,000 (88,850 miles)
Saturn	9.5	times larger	120,500 (74,900 miles)
Uranus	4	times larger	51,100 (31,750 miles)
Neptune	3.75	times larger	49,500 (30,800 miles)
Pluto	5.5	times smaller	2390 (1485 miles)

(Earth is 12,750 kilometres (7920 miles) across.)

Distance

Planet	*Distance from Sun*	
Jupiter	778 million kilometres	(483 million miles)
Saturn	1427 million kilometres	(887 million miles)
Uranus	2871 million kilometres	(1784 million miles)
Neptune	4498 million kilometres	(2795 million miles)
Pluto	5906 million kilometres	(3670 million miles)

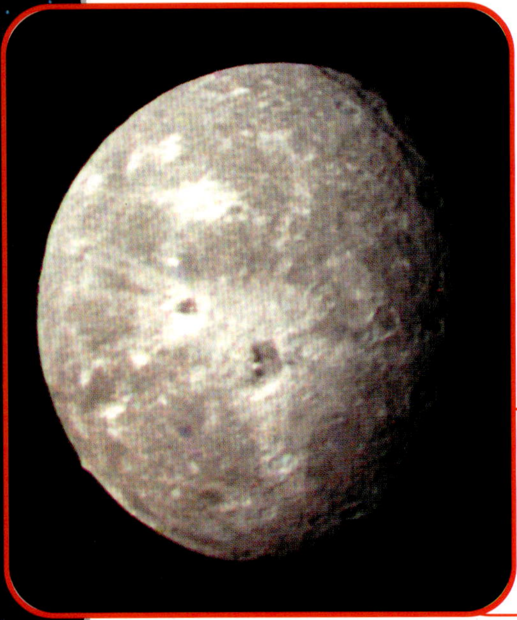

Orbit

Planet	*Time to orbit the Sun once*
Jupiter	12 years
Saturn	29 and a half years
Uranus	84 years
Neptune	165 years
Pluto	248 years

(Earth takes 1 year to orbit the Sun.)

Oberon, one of the moons of Uranus has an icy surface, covered with craters.

This image shows Pluto's true colour. The image looks blurred because it is made up of many smaller images put together. It is difficult for scientists to get a clear image of Pluto because it is so far away from Earth.

Number of known moons

Planet	*Moons*
Jupiter	At least 28
Saturn	At least 30
Uranus	At least 21
Neptune	At least 8
Pluto	1

Spin

Planet	*Time to spin around once on its axis*
Jupiter	9 hours and 55 minutes
Saturn	10 hours and 39 minutes
Uranus	17 hours and 14 minutes
Neptune	16 hours and 7 minutes
Pluto	153 hours
(Earth	24 hours)

Numbers
One thousand is written as 1000. One million is 1,000,000 and one billion is 1,000,000,000.

Glossary

astronomer scientist who studies objects in space, such as planets and stars

atmosphere layers of gases that surround a planet

axis imaginary line about which a planet or moon spins

chemical substance that is used or produced in a chemical process

comet small, icy object made of gas and dust, which orbits the Sun

crater bowl-shaped hole made on the surface of a planet or moon by a rocky object from space crashing into it

disc flat plate-shaped object

erupt burst or force out violently

gas substance that is not solid or a liquid. Oxygen is an example of a gas. It is in the air all around us and we need it to be able to breathe.

gas planets Jupiter, Saturn, Uranus and Neptune are the four gas planets

gravity force that pulls all objects towards the surface of the Earth, or any other planet, moon or star

helium the second lightest gas

hurricane very strong storm where winds blow at high speeds

hydrogen the lightest gas, and the most common one in space

methane colourless gas with an oily smell

microscopic something so small that it can only be seen using a microscope

mission job that a spacecraft does, or journey that it makes

moon small object that moves around a planet

myth old stories told to explain how something came to be

nebulae clouds of gas and dust in space. New stars are made in some nebulae.

particles very tiny amounts or pieces of a substance

planet large object moving around a star. Earth is a planet.

Poles points due North and South that mark the ends of an invisible line, called the axis, about which a planet, moon or star spins

probe unmanned spacecraft used to explore planets and moons

raw materials materials that are found in nature, that have not been man-made

scale model model showing the relative size of objects compared against each other

solar system group of nine planets and other objects orbiting the Sun

spacecraft man-made vehicle that travels beyond Earth and into space

telescope device for looking at objects that are far away, usually in the sky or in space

volcano opening in a planet's surface through which hot liquid rock is thrown up

Further reading

Exploring the Solar System: Jupiter, Giles Sparrow (Heinemann Library, 2001)

Exploring the Solar System: Saturn, Giles Sparrow (Heinemann Library, 2001)

Exploring the Solar System: Uranus, Neptune & Pluto, Giles Sparrow (Heinemann Library, 2001)

How the universe works, Heather Couper and Nigel Henbest (Dorling Kindersley, 1999)

Index